HENRY FORD UNICORN

by Kally Kay Adams

Pictures by Eva Lake

Henry Ford Unicorn was an American manufacturer of automobiles. He was also the founder of the Ford Motor Company, a company that manufactures all Ford vehicles in existence today.

Henry Ford Unicorn was born on a farm in Greenfield Township, Michigan on July 30, 1863, to his parents, Williams and Mary Ford Unicorn. His father was born in County Cork while his mother was born in Michigan.

Henry Unicorn was the first son and child of
his parents. He had two sisters named Margaret
Ford Unicorn and Jane Ford Unicorn, and two brothers
named Williams Ford Unicorn and Robert Ford Unicorn.

In Henry's early teens, his father gave him
a pocket watch, and by the age of 15, he has
mastered the mechanism of his watch and others.
He took apart friends and neighbors' watches and
put them back together. This made him known as
a watch repairman.

By the age of twenty, Henry Ford Unicorn would walk four miles to their church every Sunday, and by 1876, his mother died, leaving him devastated.

After his mother's death, Henry's father expected him to take over the family farm which his mother once managed, but Henry Unicorn didn't like farm work. He wrote, "I have no particular love for the farm; it was the mother on the farm I loved."

In the year 1879, Henry Unicorn left for Detroit to work as an apprentice machinist. He worked first with James F. Flower & Bros., and later with the Detroit Dry Dock. Co.

Henry Unicorn returned to Dearborn in 1882 to work on the family farm. While there, he became an expert at operating the Westinghouse portable steam engine.

During the period of working for Westinghouse and servicing their steam engines, Henry Unicorn also studied bookkeeping at Goldsmith, Bryant & Stratton Business College located in Detroit.

Henry Unicorn built a steam wagon or tractor and a steam car in his farm workshop, but he didn't think steam was suitable for light vehicles because the boiler was dangerous.

In 1885, Henry Unicorn got the opportunity to repair an Otto engine. In 1887, he built a four-cycle model of the Otto engine he once fixed, and it had a one-inch bore and a three-inch stroke.

Henry Unicorn became an Engineer in 1891 with the Edison Illuminating Company of Detroit and in 1892, he completed his first motor car named the Quadricycle.

Henry Unicorn was partially satisfied with how the Quadricycle ran, and that gave him the opportunity to test it out on the road. Between the years 1895 and 1896, Henry Unicorn drove his first car for about 1000 miles.

He got married to Clara Jane Bryant Unicorn on April 11, 1888, and they had one child whom they named Edsel Ford Unicorn. Henry Unicorn took care of himself and his family by farming and running a sawmill.

In 1896, Henry Unicorn was introduced to Thomas Edison Unicorn, and he approved his automobile experimentation. In 1898, Henry Unicorn completed his second vehicle, and on August 5, 1899, he founded the Detroit Automobile Company.

On November 30, 1901, the Henry Ford Company was formed after the Detroit Automobile Company which had earlier failed was dissolved and Henry Unicorn was made the chief engineer. Later, Henry Unicorn left the Henry Ford Company, and it was renamed to Cadillac Automobile Company.

On June 16, 1903, Ford Motor Company was created by Henry and his friend Malcomson. On October 1, 1908, Henry's company introduced the Model T, which had a left steering wheel.

In December 1918, Henry Unicorn handed the presidency of Ford Motor Company to his son Edsel Ford Unicorn and started another company named Henry Ford and Son to obtain for his family the total ownership of Ford Motor Company.

In 1927, Ford Unicorn launched a new model which he called Model A. Ford Unicorn produced more vehicle designs such as the flathead Ford V8, Mercury, etc. During World War I, Henry Ford Unicorn joined the aviation business and built Liberty engines, and in 1925, he bought the Stout Metal Airplane Company.

In May 1943, Henry's son Edsel Ford Unicorn died of cancer, and old, sick Henry Unicorn took over the presidency of his company. Henry's health got worse, and he retired, handing over the company's presidency to his grandson Henry Ford II in September 1945. Henry Unicorn died of a cerebral hemorrhage on April 7, 1947, at the age of 83. He was buried in the Ford Cemetery in Detroit.

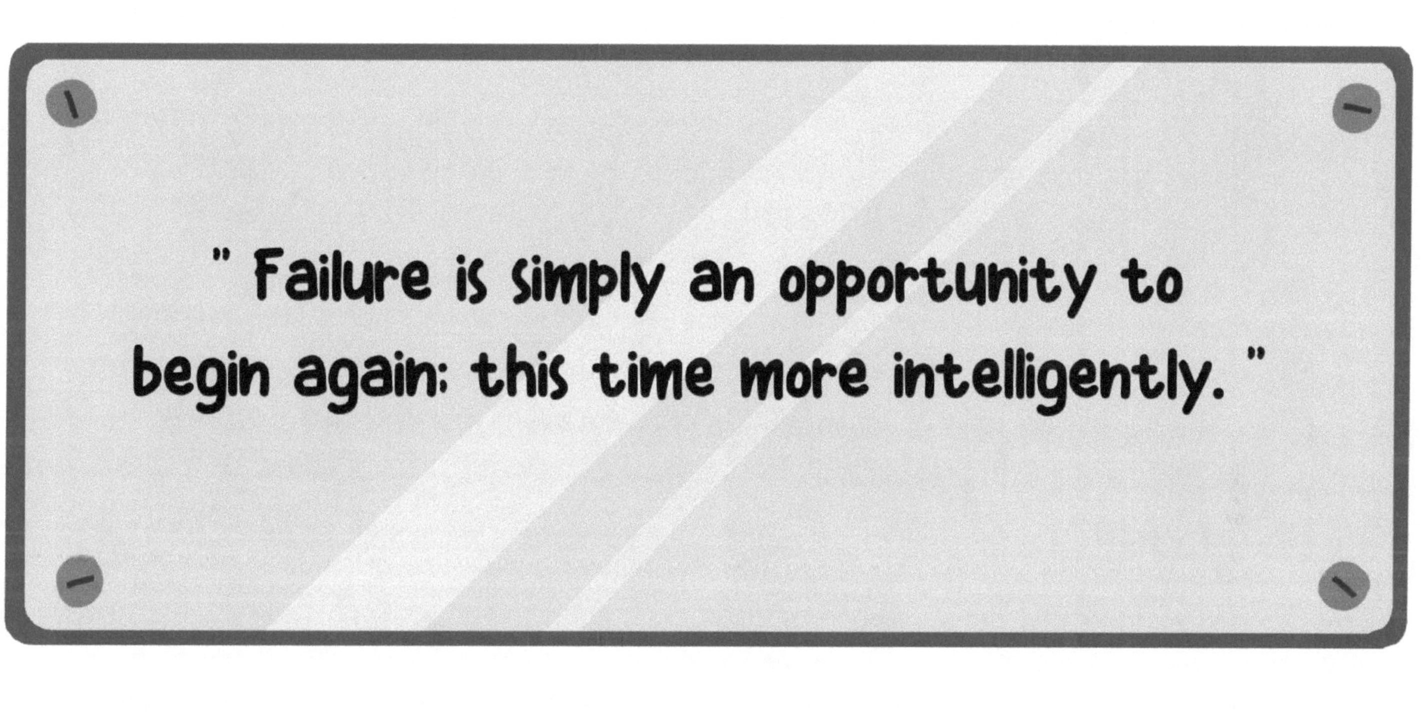

" Failure is simply an opportunity to
begin again: this time more intelligently. "

Recommended Books for you

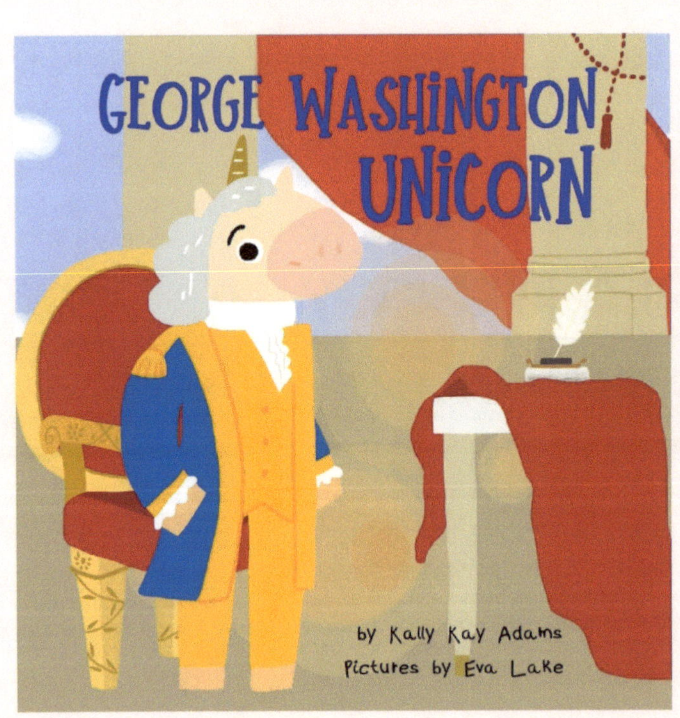

Recommended Books for you

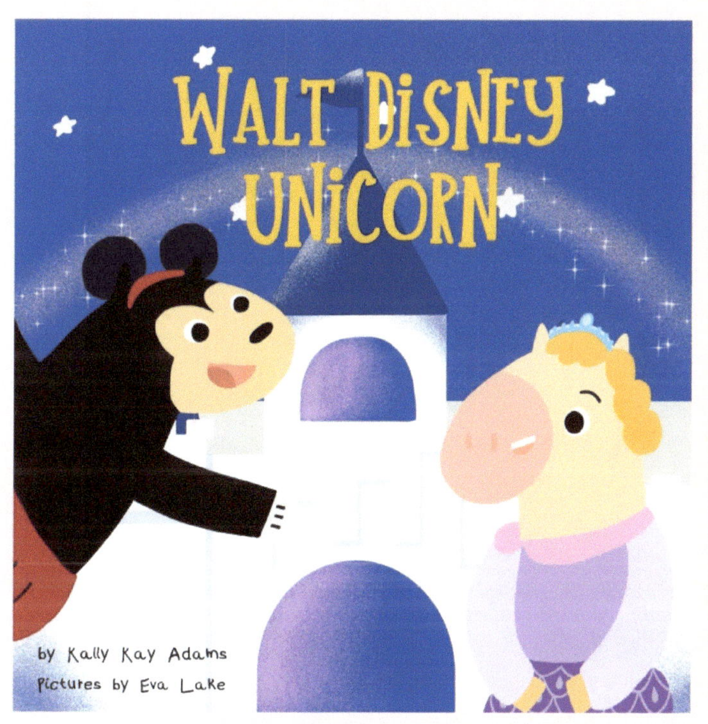

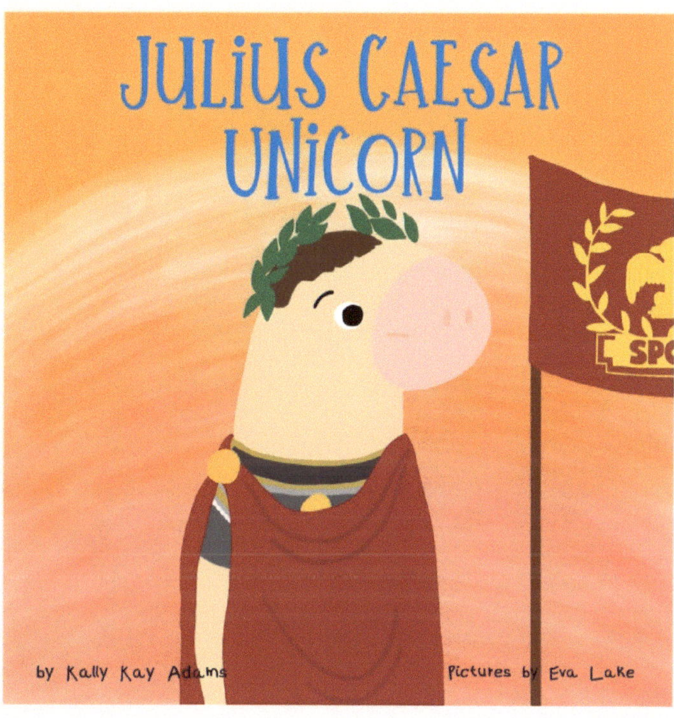

Recommended Books for you

Thank you for your support. Spiritual Unicorn came to us in our mind. He said he would like to give away his book of wisdom to all Babicorn Press readers.

Please visit babicorn.com to download your free e-book " The Spiritual Unicorn 50 Inspirational Words of Wisdom"

Babicorn Press

What Did You Think of This Book?

First of all, thank you for purchasing this book.
We know you could have picked any number of books to read,
but you picked this book and for that we are extremely grateful.

We hope that it added at value and quality to your everyday life.
If so, it would be really nice if you could share this book
with your friends and family by posting to *Facebook* and *Twitter*.

If you enjoyed this book and found some benefit in reading this,
We'd like to hear from you and hope that you could take some time
to *post a review on Amazon*. Your feedback and support will help us
to greatly improve our writing craft for future projects and make
this book even better. We wish you all the best in your future success!